FINDING GOD ALIVE!

Reclaiming the Life in the Stories of God
through
Communication and Embodiment Skills

ELIZABETH ADKISSON

Copyright
ISBN: 978-0-359-85221-5
October 26, 2016

CONTENTS

PREFACE 5

THE COMMUNICATION LOOP 7

THE COMMUNICATION LOOP WITH AN AUDIENCE 9
    Establishing Communication Loops 9
    Eye Contact 10
    Being Heard 10
    Being Seen 11
    Using Gestures and Movement 13
    Being Understood 17

EMBODIMENT OF CHARACTERS IN A STORY 24
    Using the Voice 24
    Using Personal Space 26
    Using Stance 27
    Using Silhouette 29
    Shifting Between Narrator and Character Silhouettes 29
    Example Silhouettes for Specific Characters 30
    Using Centers of Energy 31
    Using Gender 36

COMMUNICATION LOOPS BETWEEN CHARACTERS 37
    The Relationship Web 37
    Story Character Point of View 37
    Switching Communication Loops in Performance 40

PARTING THOUGHTS 43
    Evaluation of Performance Choices 43
    Finding God Alive 44

APPENDICES 45

PREFACE

Part of the blessing and pleasure of telling biblical stories is that they link us with the old, old story that gives meaning to our lives and provides a steady base for living that the current speed of life cannot obliterate. For 30+ years I labored in dark theatre spaces to direct plays and teach actors the wide range of performance skills needed to support their art. I went into these spaces because I wanted to say something about life and the way we live it. Without my recognizing what he was doing, God blessed my work in colleges, a fine arts school, and semi-professional theatres. When I retired, I came back into the light of day and to the realization that God's hand had been on me without my awareness of, or my gratitude for, his support.

"Retooling" is a catchword for our times as we live longer and find ourselves trying to survive in a world that moves faster and faster. Now that God has given me his story to tell, I feel as if my past was a training ground to prepare me for this work. Storytelling is not acting, *per se*, and telling biblical stories is a far cry from staging a dramatic work. However, there are methods of approaching acting that can help a storyteller increase the effectiveness of bringing an audience into the story and making it come to life for them. What follows is an effort to apply the tools of my former trade to my new trade. I hope that this effort can benefit other biblical storytellers, particularly those coming from other disciplines into storytelling.

The work of two other teachers has provided me with a base of knowledge from which I have worked for many years and from which I continue to draw. Arthur Lessac, who died in 2011 at age 101, published *The Use and Training of the Human Voice* in 1967. In the early 1970s I trained with this amazing man. His legacy of kinesthetic voice and body training lives through **The Lessac Training and Research Institute**, lessacinstiture.org or www.lessacinstitute.com. In 1978 Robert Cohen published *Acting Power*, the theatre's response to quantum physics. It turned the work of Stanislavsky inside out for me and made far more practical sense of the acting process.

I especially thank Dr. Tracy Radosevic, Dean of the Academy for Biblical Storytelling, for her excellent guidance and support in the development of this resource. Phil Ruge-Jones and Dennis Dewey have been so generous in their support, as well. The photography is by Jean Lambkin. My appreciation also goes to friends Harry Yeates and Debra Gates for proofing.

The performance guidelines offered in this booklet are not my own so much as they are what I have gleaned from laboring in the field of theatre. I use these guidelines in my own storytelling, and feedback from audiences indicates that they are working to enrich my storytelling. I hope that you will find these approaches of use in your storytelling.

Elizabeth Adkisson

THE COMMUNICATION LOOP

Biblical storytellers want to connect to the life in God's story to share it with others in a way that makes it alive and engaging. Storytelling requires a communication loop to be established between the teller and the listener(s). All that is necessary to establish a communication loop is the desire to communicate. In storytelling, a loop is established between the teller and *each* audience member.

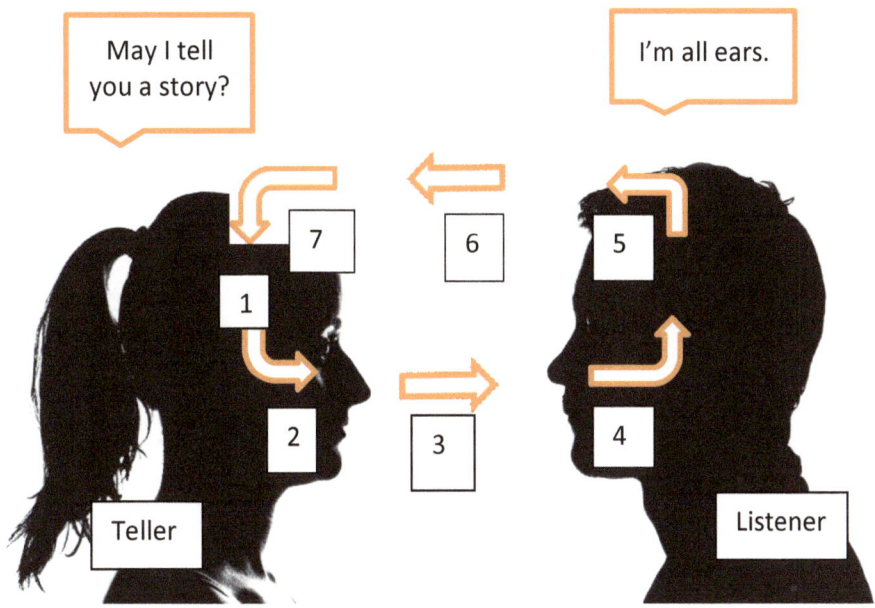

1. The teller wishes to communicate.

2. What she sees in her mind and feels internally is transmitted.

3. The transmission package includes vocal, eye, facial and body expressions and travels through space.

4. The information in the package is received by the listener's eyes, ears and body.

5. The information is processed internally and a response is formed.

6. The listener's response is transmitted to the teller.
   The response may be verbal ("amen") or non-verbal (a nod, a smile, a laugh, a scowl).

7. The response is received by the teller.

A new response is then formed by the teller, influenced by the listener's response. The loop repeats until communication ends.

The teller may be encouraged to continue because the response is what she desired or the teller might adapt, or adjust the communication, because the response is not what she desired.

Undesired responses from listeners may include, but not be limited to:
- coughing or clearing of throats
- restless movements
- people leaving
- lack of eye contact
- an unexpected laugh
- looks of confusion
- looks of disapproval
- no response
- requests to a neighbor to repeat what the teller said

The first questions, to be addressed in the face of undesired responses, concern the material selected for the performance. Was it appropriate for the specific audience? Did the delivery honor the cultural and theological orientation of the audience? Full consideration of these questions is beyond the scope of this resource, which is focused instead on actual performances of appropriate content.

If responses are not the ones desired, what other questions should the teller ask himself?

1. Am I being heard?

2. Am I being seen?

3. Am I attempting to reach and affect the listener(s)?

4. Am I making enough eye contact?

5. Are my body and voice supporting my efforts?

6. Are my words being clearly delivered?

Reviewing past problem areas while preparing future presentations is the chief opportunity to improve one's skills. The skill of making adjustments while speaking to an audience is one that only develops over time and with experience.

It is hoped that discussions and suggested experiments in the rest of this book will open doors for improvement and reveal possible solutions.

THE COMMUNICATION LOOP WITH AN AUDIENCE

> *Performance venues differ, of course, but in all venues **the performer needs to be sure that the entire audience is visible to him and that all he does is visible to the entire audience.***

ESTABLISHING COMMUNICATION LOOPS

Unless the teller makes a conscious and committed effort to form a partnership with the listener(s), functioning communication loops are unlikely to form. Whatever the teller is saying becomes noise or the background to the listeners' personal thoughts or it becomes mere entertainment from which the listener can easily disconnect. A teller almost hopes that the listener is internally saying that memorable line from the movie *Taxi Driver*, "Are you talking to *me*?"

A teller, of course, has no control over the listener. However, the teller can influence the listener to set aside her resistance and open the pathway for communication. The teller is asking permission of every listener in the audience to share a communication loop with him. Even if this invitation exists only in the mind of the teller, it becomes a powerful impulse within the teller to establish a loop. Likewise, it would be wonderful if every listener actually said to the teller, "Please, share with me." The teller, however, can approach the situation as if every listener has actually granted her that permission.

The beginning encounter between teller and listener is critical and should be handled thoughtfully. A teller can prepare the material to be communicated with the greatest of care;

but, unless he prepares himself to share and the audience to receive, there will not be a strong communication loop. It is the commitment to communication, doing it skillfully and believing that it will be received, that gives the teller the will, courage and hope to move forward.

EYE CONTACT

If the teller is not actually looking at the audience during a performance, then the teller is severing the part of the communication loop that supplies her feedback from the listeners.

One sign that both parties in the loop are willing for the communication to happen is that they can look at each other (make eye contact). The teller needs to be willing to look at everyone even though, in truth, that rarely happens in an audience of listeners, especially in a large auditorium.

When the teller speaks directly to the audience, he is making eye contact with the various individuals in that audience. When the teller speaks as one character in the story to another character, he is making eye contact with the audience as if he were seeing the character to whom he is speaking sitting in every seat in the audience. The audience is both a witness to a communication and a participant in the communication loops between story characters. Further on we deal with the placement of story characters in relationship to the audience to optimize this duality.

BEING HEARD

The trick to communication is to attempt to genuinely be heard and *to affect* every listener at every distance and angle from the teller. If a teller's communication is not received internally by a listener, then there is no communication loop with that listener.

Just increasing volume misses the point. Yes, a teller may find that when she adjusts to cover the physical space between her and her listeners that she may speak louder, but having the listeners internalize the story is the point. It is more a matter of attitude and desire to communicate. If a teller has any doubts about sharing with listeners, those doubts will break down communication. The doubts may arise from lack of preparation, lack of confidence, self-monitoring, or failure to adjust to the physical performance space.

Being heard is also improved by the teller's receptivity and ability to adjust to audience responses. Remember that the teller's reception is part of the communication loop. The success of communication hangs on the moment-to-moment response of the listener(s). Even if there is not an actual sound or movement coming from the listeners, the teller can sense a connection.

In a performance space, the teller needs to make certain that the vibrations of his voice can be felt returning to him from the walls and surfaces of the space. Even when using a microphone, the teller needs to check that his voice is actually travelling back to him. Once an audience enters the space, their bodies will absorb sound. Further adjustment may be necessary after a couple of words have been spoken to the audience.

BEING SEEN

Our eyes take in information faster than our ears.

Being seen is linked to being heard. A great deal of human communication comes through lip reading, facial cues and eye contact, particularly if the teller is not wearing a microphone. Therefore, people receive and understand a great deal more of the communication if they can see the teller's eyes, watch her facial expressions and see her lips move.

If the teller is not in the light, the listeners' ability to understand what is being communicated will be diminished because the teller's features will be difficult to see. Unfortunately, many of the spaces that biblical storytellers use have very, very poor lighting. The teller needs to make every effort to find light and stay in it.

The teller must get into the light or…

the light will take focus away from the teller.

If the teller is not in the light, but there is light in the performance space, the light will upstage the teller (people will look at the light more than the teller). The same problem arises when a teller uses a projection screen while speaking. If the teller needs the focus on him, he must avoid trying to compete for attention with a video behind him or above him. Unless the teller has carefully timed speaking to occur during lulls in the video, he will have difficulty drawing the listeners' eyes away from the screen.

The teller is better connected to an audience if each member of the audience can see the teller's face. Therefore, the teller needs to consciously make her face available to as much of the audience as possible for as much time as possible. If the audience seating wraps around the performance space, then the teller will have to make sure that all of the audience has an opportunity to see crucial facial expressions and gestures.

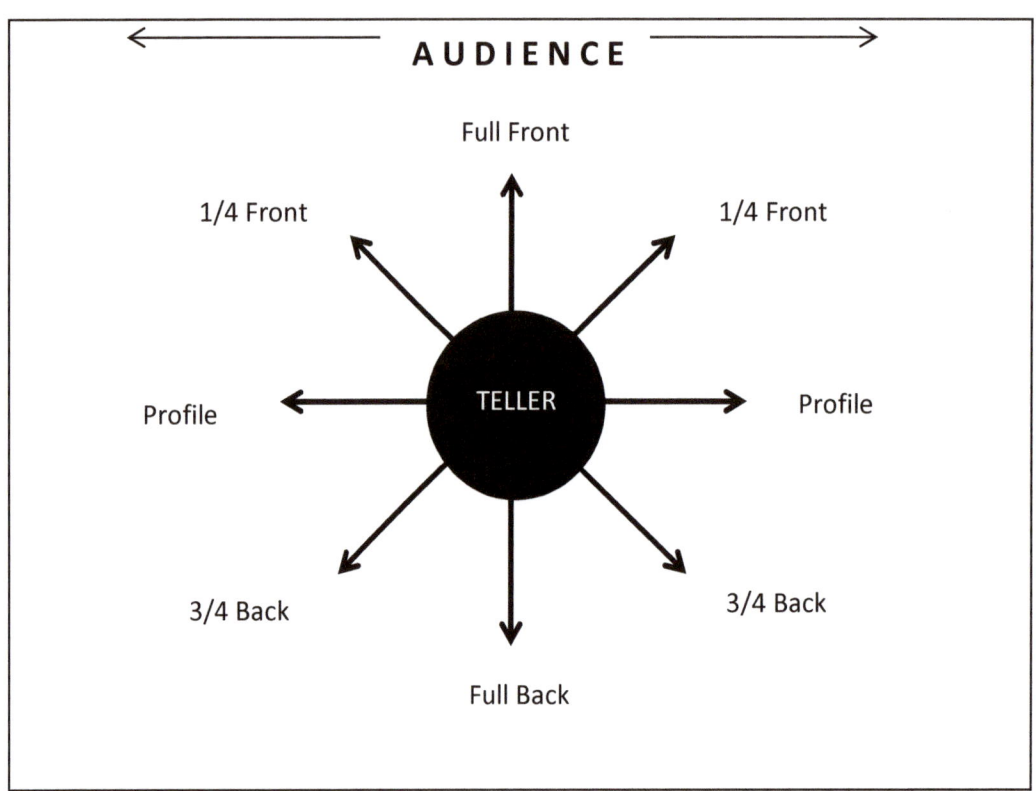

Performer Body Directions in Relationship to an Audience

As a performer turns away from full front, he usually begins to exclude some of the audience. The more he turns, the more members are excluded. Consideration needs to be given regarding when to turn, how much to turn, how long to stay turned and when to change from one degree of a turn to another. Once he passes a 1/4 turn, a teller has to make adjustments, such as holding a significant expression as he turns back towards full front or even on to 1/4 in the opposite direction. Fortunately, the human head swivels on the neck to help make the necessary adjustments to maintain communication loops.

It is important to remember that the teller is not on a set and is not bound by a stage setting. Therefore, the teller is free to place whoever and whatever needs to be in front of her to tell the story. Who and what is in front of the teller keeps changing as the story unfolds. Since a teller does not use actual props and furniture, in most cases, a character can place objects without concern for where these things might be placed in reality.

USING GESTURES AND MOVEMENT

Many people "talk with their hands," but a teller needs to make *conscious* choices regarding gestures. One sign of being unconscious about gesturing is a hand moving in the same way over and over with word after word. The repetition establishes a rhythm that may help the teller remember the words but it can distract the listeners by drawing the eyes away from what is being said or contradicting what is being said. Remember that the eye receives information faster than the ear.

The most effective gestures are those that capture the emotional or psychological tone described in the words. Sometimes gestures are utilitarian such as emphasizing where "there" is as opposed to "here." But gestures are most helpful and expressive when they support the underlying atmosphere or feeling of the words. They paint pictures in the listeners' minds. They need to have meaning to the audience within their culture.

"...and they were filled by the Holy Spirit."

Parallel gestures occur when one uses both hands in the same way or both arms bent at the same angle. Parallel gestures need to be a conscious choice for a purpose. For example: Hebrew prayer might be indicated by raising both hands on bent arms to either side of the head and moving them in unison while bobbing the upper body. If parallel gestures are overused or become a teller's default choice, they become less effective and uninteresting. Using only one hand or arm or putting arms or hands at different heights and angles is more artistic and keeps audiences more engaged.

Parallel gesture with slightly different heights

Non-parallel gesture

Extending one's arm fully makes a stronger gesture than extending it only part of the distance from the torso. If the teller needs to be forceful, demanding, powerful, or fully committed, then the arm needs to extend to its limit.

Open hand on bent elbow

Open hand on extended arm

A hand gesture with a bent elbow makes a different statement from the same gesture at the end of an extended arm. A bent elbow with hand open might simply soften the effect of the spoken words but it could indicate that the gesture is being used to negate what is being spoken. For example, in the photos above, imagine the words, "All this will be yours." The gesture in the left photo could signal that "all" is a far lesser amount than the gesture in the right photo indicates; OR, the gesture in the left photo could signal that the "all" is far less willingly given than it is in the right photo.

Speed, or amount of energy expended, in executing a gesture changes the affect of the gesture.

Experiment: Select a gesture such as a hand turned palm upward. Try using it with:

- a bent elbow
- an extended arm
- an arm extended slowly
- an arm extended quickly
- an arm extend with little energy
- an arm extended with great energy.

Each gesture communicates something different. You will feel that and so will your listeners through their kinesthetic sense.

If your hands and gestures obscure your face, communication is diminished.

Body and mouth *covered* by a gesture diminishes communication.

Body and mouth *not covered* by a gesture enhances communication.

In order to remain visible to the audience while gesturing toward something on the left of his body, the teller should use his left arm; to gesture toward something on the right of his body, the teller should use his right arm.

Sweeping gestures (ones that travel through space) do not stop in front of the body or face and, therefore, keep communication open. As pictured, if the arm in this case quickly sweeps on across to end on the right of the teller's body, communication will not be diminished because the teller's face will quickly be revealed.

Sweeping Gesture

Unconscious movement (particularly of the feet) is distracting and counter-productive. It does convey nervousness, if that is what is desired; otherwise, feet and body movements should be purposeful and judicious. Everyone has habitual movements and gestures. The teller needs to become aware of her default settings and replace them with movements and gestures that are supportive of each story told. The subject of performance evaluation is addressed on page 43.

Taking a first step from a standing position needs a plan. When moving from a position facing the audience to travel to your right (whether for one step or several), leading out with the right foot keeps the body open to the audience; but, leading out with the left foot crossing the right covers the body and is awkward physically. For ease of movement, if you are moving to the left, start with the left foot; if you are moving to the right, start with the right foot.

To step to your right, begin with the right foot to avoid crossing your body and looking awkward.

Stepping out to your right with your left foot is awkward and unbalanced.

A teller's facial expression and body language can contradict her words and intended meaning.

If your body says one thing and your voice another, the hearer believes your body.

If your face says one thing and your voice another, the hearer believes your face.

Note: A teller might *consciously* choose to use this principle to convey that a story's character is not sincere or is lying. The problem occurs when the teller *unconsciously* sabotages the communication and ends up saying something he did not mean. Avoiding this problem is a matter of using video or a practice audience to get the necessary feedback. Performance evaluation methods are discussed on page 43.

BEING UNDERSTOOD

American English tellers, as a group, tend to be lazy with enunciation and do not fully execute all the producible sounds of each word they speak. This is a matter beyond, though influenced, by dialects. Dialects should not become an excuse for not trying to improve oral communication. Unfortunately, clearing up speech habits is far from easy. Once a person has spoken in a certain manner for years, it takes at least a couple of years of daily practice and tutoring to replace the ingrained habits.

Particularly for someone performing for a wide range of listeners, clearing up unproductive speech habits is worth the effort. Without awareness of how speech is produced in the human body, how it interplays with breath, how it is shaped by the positions of the lips, teeth and tongue, and how it resonates, one cannot gain control and flexibility of vocal delivery. The range of speech choices needed to fully convey something as intricate as an oral story is rich with possibilities if one knows what to do.

There are many systems of vocal training available. Having taught vocal skills to acting students for many years, I would recommend trying one that is built on how vocal production <u>feels</u> as it is happening in the body rather than one that is built on trying to produce sounds from written symbols or relying upon hearing as one speaks. The problem with relying on written symbols (such as the International Phonetic Alphabet) is the difficulty of accurately translating the symbols into sounds without adequate information on how the sound is to be produced.

The problem with relying on hearing as one speaks is that the human brain simultaneously receives two sets of vibrations in the hearing process: air and bone. When speaking, the speaker receives a combination of sound waves through the air to his ear <u>and</u> sound waves coming by vibration through his bones. When a person first hears himself on a vocal recording, he does not think that is how he sounds. However, it <u>is</u> how he sounds to his listeners who are receiving his communication only through sound waves traveling through the air, just as the recording devise does.

Arthur Lessac developed a system for training the voice by focusing on the body actions required to produce the sounds. I trained with him and know his book *The Use and Training of the Human Voice* to be an excellent guide. It can be approached alone, but an instructor/coach would be more than a little helpful. There is information available online about his institute and for finding Lessac-trained and certified teachers (lessacinstitute.org).

While biblical storytellers perform translations, investigation into the original meanings and nuances of Hebrew and Greek words is illuminating for giving emphasis in the appropriate places and in the appropriate ways. Interlinear Hebrew and Greek biblical texts are available online, as are a host of translations. Good translations can expose a repetition of sounds that can prove beneficial in learning and communicating a story. The Network of Biblical Storytellers, International, when working together in performing, uses the New Revised Standard Version. When selecting a story to learn, it is helpful to consult many translations before selecting the one to be told.

After all the work is done preparing what is to be said, clear delivery of the teller's words is absolutely essential. There are many important aspects of vocal delivery.

Sample text Luke 8:2-3:

The twelve were with him, as well as some women who had been cured of evil spirits and infirmities: Mary, called Magdalene, from whom seven demons had gone out, and Joanna, the wife of Herod's steward Chuza, and Susanna, and many others who provided for them out of their resources.

1. Organize the material into complete thoughts.

    Sample text: The punctuation of the text leads to the understanding that twelve men and a list of women were with Jesus at this time. The colon preceding the name of the first woman leads to the further understanding that all of the people listed after Susanna are women. Two of the woman's names are followed by further explanation of their identities. It could be understood that the original listeners would be familiar with these women but would need to be told which Mary had been the one cured and which Joanna.

2. Use the punctuation as a guide for pauses and stops.

    Sample text: The colon should produce a longer pause than the commas. The pauses help organize the material for the listener and give the teller time to make matters clear.

3. Practice those hard-to-say names and words until they feel natural.

    Sample text: Magdalene is probably familiar but a teller might want to know how to pronounce Chuza. Online sites for pronunciation of Bible names provide both International Phonetic Alphabet written explanations and audio pronunciation guides.

4. Use consonants where they are available for use.

English is not just a jumble of vowel sounds. Consonants are necessary for precise meaning and they offer far more "vocal music" than vowel sounds. Arthur Lessac used the image of an orchestra to teach the consonant possibilities. There are strings, woodwinds, tympani, horns and specialty instruments available. Plus, there are all the different ways in which those instruments can be played. Playing consonant sounds as if they are emerging from a musical instrument encourages more expressive speech. Meaning, mood, motivation and an increased range of actions can all come through the consonants.

In most cases (except for extreme emphasis of each word), words in a sentence are not produced as independent units. *I-did-not-do-it; I-did-something-else.* Consonants frequently function in combinations that, unless understood and used, make it possible to overuse them and to sound stilted. The following is grounded in the Lessac method.

When a word ending in a vowel is followed by one beginning in a consonant, the two words can flow together with no break: I did.

When a word ending in a consonant is followed by one beginning with a vowel, the final consonant of the first word become the beginning sound of the second word: something else.

(Note: "ng" is a single sound and is not produced like an "n" + "g.")

When two consonants come together, either within a word or in a two-word unit, there are several considerations. If the consonants are not related in any way (not produced in the same or nearly the same way as each other), then the first one can receive extra energy (can be played as if it were an instrument in an orchestra as mentioned above).

If the first consonant is one that can be played in a sustained way, then it can be played and linked to the second: didn't or something.

(Note: In the second word, the "e" is silent so the "m" and the "th" come together. The "m" is a sustainable sound that is continued until the "th" is produced.)

If the first consonant is one that can be played in a percussive way, then it can be played and linked to the second: did something.

A final consonant before a pause is automatically in a playable position: it, and something. The "t" is percussive and the "ng" is sustainable.

When two consonants come together that are in some way related (produced in the same way or in nearly the same way as each other), the first is prepared only and the second is produced: **didn't do**.

To produce both the "t" and the following "d" would cause an unnecessary pause.

In the same word there is an example of "d" preceding "n." These two consonants are considered semi-related in this direction because the tip of the tongue goes up to the gum ridge to prepare a "d" in the same way that it does for an "n". The difference is that to produce a "d" the tip of the tongue has to pop off the gum ridge. Since the tip will have to return immediately to the same position and remain in place to produce an "n," a gap would result if the speaker tried to fully execute both sounds. Therefore, the flow of the thought is kept intact by letting the tongue prepare the "d" but go on to produce the "n:" **didn't**.

There is also an unwritten "w" between "do" and "it." Producing that "w" will allow for completion of the phrase with no breaks in sound: **do(w)it**.

The phrase would have the following consonant action:
I didn't do(w)it; I did something el se.

(Note: The "l" and "s" are two separate sounds in the final word.)

In places where consonant sounds end sentences or phrases, they often go unused. For example, final "d" and "t" sounds are easily lost because they are not transmitted unless the tip of the tongue *pops down* from the gum ridge. If the tongue is left up on the gum ridge, there is no "d" or "t" produced.

Experiment: Say the following phrases ending in "d" or "t" first leaving the tongue touching the gum ridge and then say it popping the tongue off the gum ridge.

        Stop that!   It's the end.

Perhaps this discussion underscores the need for training by a coach. (See Appendix B for further coverage.) Once consonant action is learned, the fun of using it is worth the effort.

5. Increase volume, not by shouting or yelling, but by ***"calling."***

Shouting and yelling are actions that produce tension in the mouth and throat. Vocal sound is not magnified by pushing sound out of the throat or by using a great deal of breath. Rather the voice is magnified in the body by using the soundwaves vibrating the bones of the face and head and letting them bounce and reverberate in the oral, sinus, head and chest cavities. Lessac refers to this process as *calling*. To do it, focus the soundwaves on the hard palate at the roof of the mouth and use a fully open oral cavity (teeth apart). If the upper lip is stretched forward as it is when producing the consonant "*y*," the face from the upper lip to the forehead becomes one side of an **inverted megaphone** magnifying the voice. It should feel as if your voice is traveling through your forehead and filling up a large room or stadium without any tension.

Instead of needing an actual megaphone to amplify the voice, use:

- the lips in the position of saying a "y" consonant,
- an open oral cavity and
- the bones of the face to form an inverted megaphone to amplify the voice.

a. *Calling* <u>to cover physical distance</u>.

Experiment: In a large open space, face a partner (so that you are closer than arm's-length from each other) and each of you say "hello." Then keep walking backwards away from each other one step at a time saying "hello" with each step.

As you get farther from each other, it might help to cup your hands around your lips as a mini-megaphone to help you remember that you want to "call" using your internal, inverted megaphone structure to keep from shouting or yelling. You should find yourself able to increase volume without effort or stress.

Keep your focus on making a side of the megaphone with your lips, open oral cavity and facial bones. Once you are as far away as possible, then reverse the process by decreasing volume each time you step toward each other.

b. *Calling* <u>to cover emotional distance</u>.

Experiment: Try to remember what it felt like to *call* over the greatest distance in the former experiment. Then try staying close to each other but *calling* as if the distance were increasing between you. You might try a simple exchange such as "I will do it" and "You won't do it." Increase your volume gradually.

Now you begin to enter the territory of calling over emotional distance. As you increase volume you will feel the use of greater energy and intensity. You might feel that you are engaged in an argument, a struggle for power, a last ditch effort to get through to someone, etc.

6. Use volume changes judiciously.

There are times when increased volume is effective and times when decreased volume is effective. The trouble comes when these are the only two choices a teller uses for emphasis.

Warning: If the pattern of loud, soft, loud, soft develops, the result is like listening to someone play with a dial on a radio. It not only causes listeners to miss words, but it becomes annoying and ineffectual. The audience stops listening.

7. Use tempo changes reasonably.

Tempo variations can be very useful to indicate changes in situation or to emphasize and give weight to words spoken.

Warning: The teller needs to give herself time to form the words, all the words, especially when the tempo is rapid. Listeners need time to receive, process, and respond to all that is being spoken to them.

8. Use silences/pauses logically.

Pauses are needed at times to signal something important has been communicated or is about to be communicated. Silence can help make transitions as a character makes adjustments to a situation.

Warning: Pauses *can* be overused and interrupt the flow of communication. Use them when they are important enough to the meaning to merit use.

9. Emphasize words with finesse.

Note: Biblical storytellers work from translations. Investigation into the original meanings of Hebrew and Greek words, along with study Bible notes and biblical commentaries is often necessary to understand what was being communicated. Good translators recognize that the sounds in the original words played a role in transmitting the intended experience of the story. Therefore, these translators attempt to choose words in the second language (among those with the same meaning) that carry a similar energy or weight as the sounds of the original language. Paying attention to the sounds of the text is another way of finding the life in the text.

Applying force or volume to emphasize a word or words is only one of *many* choices and, arguably, the least subtle. Of course, not being subtle might be just what works in some cases.

Other means of emphasizing words include:
- change of tempo from the surrounding words
- extending or manipulating the vowel or consonant sounds within a word
- using changes in volume
- using pauses around words (This practice can be disruptive to the flow of the speech, so be careful.)

Experiment: Using the following verses from Psalm 24, try out the following adjustments:

- Tempo variations – entire verse, selected words or phrases
- Pause placement and duration – punctuation and stress pauses
- Volume changes – entire verse, selected words or phrases
- Extension of the sounds of the vowel and consonants
- Narrative style – mystery, romance, joke, fairy tale, tragedy

See how much variety you can discover and how you can find surprising ways to vary how words are emphasized. Playing possibilities are limited only by one's imagination.

> *The earth is the LORD's and all that is in it,*
> *the world, and those who live in it;*
> *for he has founded it on the seas,*
> *and established it on the rivers.*

10. Use the instant before speech begins.

In a communication loop there is a moment right before a person speaks that reflects the internal monologue or internal image that formed the thought about to be spoken. There can emerge a look in the eyes, an expression on the face, a bit of breath, a slight change in posture, etc., that sets into play the atmosphere in which the speaker launches his words. Great use can be made of that moment if the teller will give himself the time to express it.

EMBODIMENT OF CHARACTERS IN A STORY

Each character in a story is unique. Pertinent information about the gender, age, status, situation, motivation and point of view of each character can be embodied by the teller when portraying each character.

All work towards embodiment of characters begins with investigating the historical, cultural, political and religious world of the story. In a biblical story, consideration can be given to the story's place in the unfolding story of God and to interpretations that may have been attached to the story through commentaries or traditions. Determining when the story was originally told, to whom it was originally told, and for what purpose can shed important light on the world expressed by the original teller. Research helps the contemporary teller to step into the world of the characters and to make informed choices for performing the story.

Choices for physically and vocally embodying characters should be based on clues discovered about each character in a story. Beyond the background research conducted, clues may by found in how other characters describe them, the things said to them, the actions they pursue, the words they speak and the attitudes they display.

Strive to make choices first from the data available in the text and the research rather than from flights of fancy or attempts to make "interesting" choices. Being uninformed can lead to inappropriate choices, possibly weakening the integrity of the text. The teller must be confident with the interpretation of each character before "walking in the character's shoes."

USING THE VOICE

There are many possible vocal choices. A character's situation, status, age, gender, point of view and motivation can all be communicated through vocal delivery. Playing with the words is important for finding the best solutions. Here are a *few* examples of choices:

Situation:
- A character *addressing a crowd* will need a large public vocal delivery to reach the crowd. This delivery would have the calling quality to cover distance.
  (See discussion on *calling*, pages 20-22, which distinguishes between calling and shouting.)
- A character in the crowd commenting to those near to her, or *one individual talking normally to another,* can use a more intimate vocal delivery.

Motivation :
- A character in an argument, or attempting to gain power in a situation, could go into calling delivery to cover the emotional distance from another character.

- A character needing to urgently influence someone may use a faster pace and more emphatic consonants.
- A character who is reluctant to be influenced might speak slower and more hesitantly or thoughtfully.

Status:
- A character of higher status may use a loftier or weightier vocal delivery over a character of a lower status.
- A character of lower status might use a softer, more hesitant vocal delivery in responding to a character of higher status.

Age:
- A character of greater age might have a slacker jaw and require more time with speech. The voice might be less vital or weaker.
- A younger character may want to rush ahead, eager to communicate and take action, thus falling over his words.

Gender:
- There is a full range in both the feminine and masculine speaking voice, although the range <u>generally</u> starts lower for the masculine voice.
- A male character may use a much lower pitch when he wishes to have power over another person. There might be gruffness or greater volume.
- A female character would generally be in a slightly higher range and softer, but the female voice in its upper ranges should be avoided because listeners tend to block out that vocal level as it becomes irritating.

USING PERSONAL SPACE

Humans have a kinesthetic sense that allows them to know how they are occupying space. Because both the teller and the audience share this same sense, the audience will gather information from their own bodies as they watch and listen to a teller. Again, the eyes gather information faster than the ears. The audience automatically feels and understands a familiar gesture executed by a teller and knows what the muscles of the facial expression are communicating.

Personal space is the area that an individual can reach with her arms and legs from a stationary position. One could say that the expression "keeping at arm's length" is another way of describing keeping something out of one's personal space. Personal space is something a person can sense without physically reaching out. A sort of bubble might be imagined encircling a body. One's space is invaded when another person moves into the area occupied by that bubble. There are, of course, moments when invasion is invited or desired and other moments when invasion creates undesireable tension or danger.

Understanding the filling of personal space is important to the storyteller's ability to bring each character, with his or her own personal space, to life. How one fills one's space affects how one stands, moves, speaks, gestures, breathes, projects an image into the world and influences others.

Experiment for sensing your own personal space:

Stand with a partner facing you.

Each of you extend an arm out so that your finger tips are about to touch between you.

Put the arms down and pay attention to the feeling that you are close to each other but not in each other's personal space.

Then step toward each other just enough to feel that you have entered each other's personal space.

Back out again and reestablish personal spaces.

Repeat this process decreasing the distance between you until you are "in each other's face."

As you continue to repeat this process, focus on how you feel at the different distances from your partner.

You might also try one partner remaining still while the other partner makes several moves in and out of the stationary partner's personal space.

Individuals fill their spaces differently by cultural norms, by habit and by situation. Habitually, some individuals fill all of their space, others fill their own space plus some space others are occupying, still others never manage to completely fill their own space fully or use very reduced space.

Situational changes in a story can cause characters to fill space differently. A character may experience a change of status, health, emotional condition or spiritual awareness during the course of a story. Once someone is healed, forgiven, victorious, defeated, that person tends to both fill his personal space differently and to see the world differently.

USING STANCE

Generally, a stance with feet parallel and shoulder-width apart makes a strong base for telling and narrating. This base is also useful for very centered characters and those clearly aligned with God. Feet together makes an unstable base and is not a useful choice, unless inebriation is to be reflected. For all other speakers in a story, the stance is the beginning of the silhouette each character.

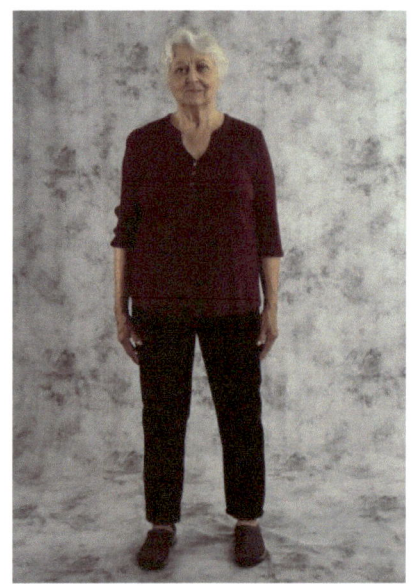

Neutral, balanced stance

Off-balance, unstable stance

Toes turned out

Toes turned in

Experiment: Try the stances pictured above and see how each makes you feel. Walk around keeping each foot in its original orientation (front and separated about 12 inches, toes turned in, toes turned out, feet too close together) to get a stronger idea of what is being projected about a person just with that base. Vary the pace and strength of each step to discover more information.

While the teller does not often walk as the various characters within a story, such experiments reveal much about what it is like to be walking in another's shoes. That is information the teller needs to fully communicate every part of the story whether or not that particular character actually walks within the course of telling the story.

USING SILHOUETTE

The silhouette is the normal outline and skeleton of a character in his or her personal space. It includes stance, skeleton, posture, angle of head, and attitude within personal space.

Consideration needs to be given to whether a character differs in attitude from others of the same station in life or other members of a family value system, etc. A character may have qualities that God has not yet revealed. For example, Samson may be big and strong but he does not fully recognize the range of his strength until God releases it to conquer the lion. He does not understand why he has this strength until he has to choose to use it to destroy Israel's enemies, even when it means self-destruction.

A range of silhouette choices and ideas can emerge from observing other people, live or in photographs and videos. Other choices might spring from one's imagination as triggered from one's research and study.

The silhouette may be a function of a situation that will change during the story. Therefore, a change in the situation during the story can alter the silhouette. People get healed, forgiven, defeated, betrayed, etc., and how they fill their space afterwards is likely to change accordingly.

Information to seek:

- What is the normal outline of this person?
- What is her normal stance?
- How does he stand, hold his head and neck?
- How does she usually hold her arms?
- How much of his personal space does he generally fill?

SHIFTING BETWEEN NARRATOR AND CHARACTER SILHOUETTES

Experiment: Once you have a silhouette that feels useful to you for a particular character, go back and forth from your own silhouette as the narrator to the character's silhouette. It helps to be subtle so that you can change back and forth quickly. You don't want to call attention to what you are doing in performance.

Try to ingrain the silhouette in your muscle memory by going into it and freezing and then going back to your silhouette. Then practice popping in and out of the silhouette several times.

With some practice, you will begin to be able to quickly project the character without having to really think about it. Slide into the silhouette just as you (as the narrator) finish introducing the character's action or speech. Not all characters begin their response with words. Frequently there are physical and vocal responses that precede spoken words.

EXAMPLE SILHOUETTES FOR SPECIFIC CHARACTERS

KING AHAB

Twice in the stories of King Ahab he is told to go have something to eat and drink. In both cases it is a dismissal or a ploy to get him out of the way while Elijah or Jezebel takes care of important business of which he is not capable. It could be useful to imagine him with an expanded stomach that is overfilled too often. His feet would be wider apart to make a wider base. He would lean slightly backward to counterbalance the weight he carries up front. Doing so could then cause him to lower his chin which might cause him to look down on others. This position could in turn drive his voice into lower pitches.

THE WIDOW OF ZAREPHATH

The widow of Zarephath has been suffering in an extended drought. She and her son are at the point of starvation and she expects them to die. Her stomach is empty and caved in. Her energy level is so low that she is dragging herself to pick up a couple of sticks. She can hardly lift her head to respond to Elijah's requests for water and bread. This silhouette is not her normal silhouette, but it is the starting silhouette for this story.

HEROD

King Herod has to focus all his mental energy when the Wise Men ask about the Messiah. He has to set a scheme and yet appear sincere. His body becomes very still as his mind darts to calculate what can be done to rid himself of this threat and yet he has to mediate this energy before the Wise Men. A slight tilt of the head making his smile crooked could illustrate his veiled cunning.

USING CENTERS OF ENERGY

Centers of energy help to activate a silhouette in a way that exposes a character's constitution, disposition, personality traits, reputation, temperament and attitude in normal and abnormal situations.

The focus in this section is to encourage activating the silhouette in order to discover meaningful gesture choices and vocal choices for each character. The use of energy centers affects breathing and vocal production. Activating energy centers for exploration can involve excessive movements or moving from place to place. Storytellers usually tell stories without relying on a great deal of movement from place to place. It is possible and important to be able to draw from the appropriate energy center to fully embody an action or a moment in a story without having to move around. Muscle memory does the work.

The main centers are the head, the chest, the stomach and the pelvis/legs. If a person's chief center of energy at one moment is the head (mental), her other centers tend to be stiller and quieter or to act in support of the dominant center by not drawing energy away or by sending extra energy in support. For example, a woman is trying to reach an important decision. The rest of her body may remain absolutely still as she thinks or her legs might pace as she thinks.

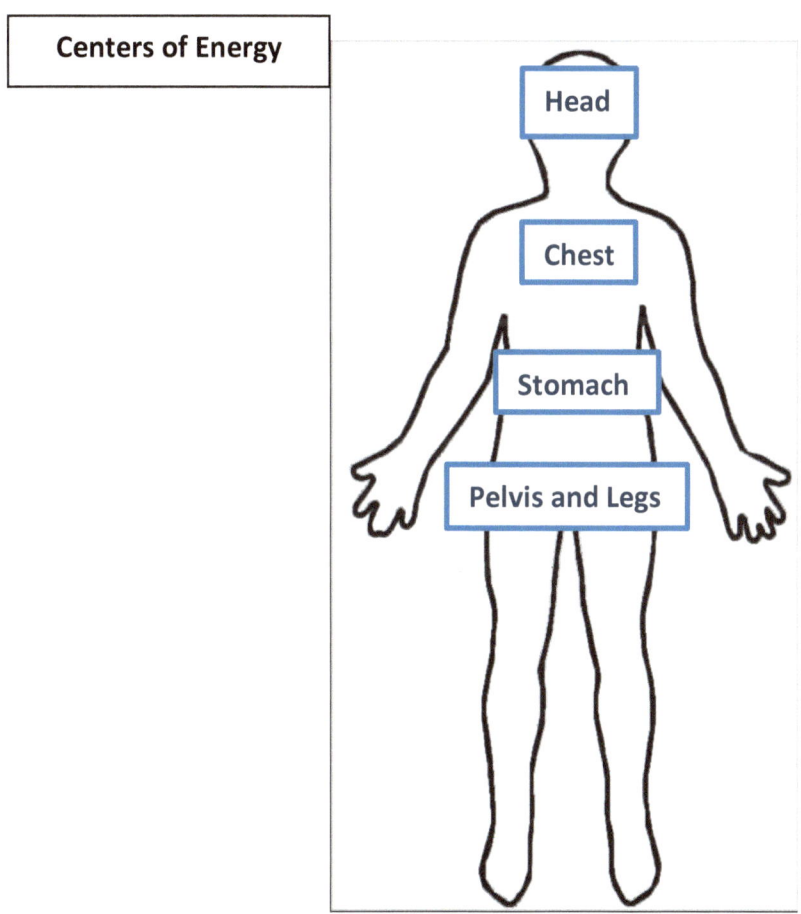

Energy from each of the four centers can be either *contracted* or *expanded*. Within either contraction or expansion there is a range of expression that can emerge.

The following examples show two images within each of the four centers. The first image from each center represents use of contracted energy and the other exhibits expanded energy. Contracted energy folds in on itself while expanded energy flows outward.

Written below the photographs are only <u>some</u> of the emotional, physical or psychological possibilities within each range.

Contracted Head Energy
confusion, fatigue, worry, obsession

Expanded Head Energy
scheming, calculation, creativity, idea formation

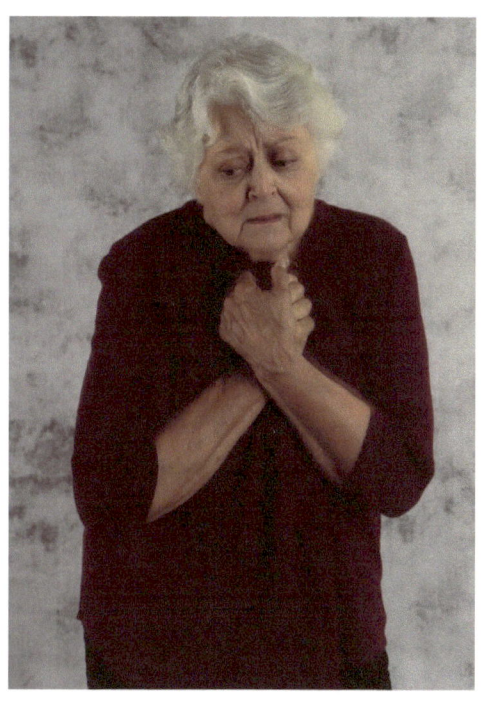

Contracted Chest Energy

defeat, apprehension, poor esteem, disappointment, sorrow, longing

Expanded Chest Energy

love, pride, courage, boldness, hope, egotism

Contracted Stomach Energy

hunger, fear, terror

Expanded Stomach Energy

satisfaction, indulgence, humor

Contracted Pelvis/Leg Energy

self-protection, stealth, caution

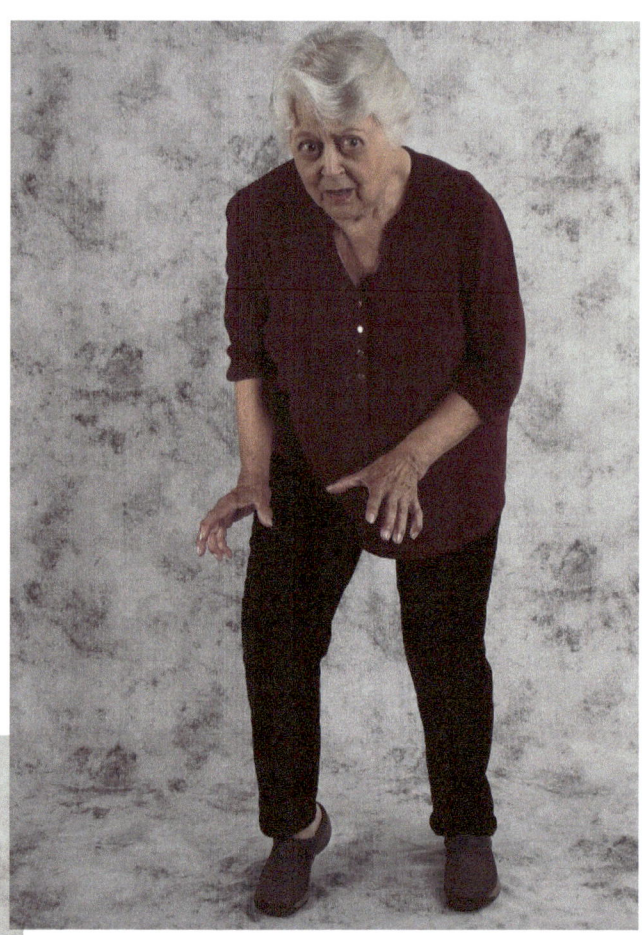

Expanded Pelvis/Leg Energy

lust, aggression, brutality

Focusing intentionally on centers of energy can help build a general silhouette for a character if his actions, or what is said about him, suggest that he habitually operates out of one center more than the others. Switching centers of energy can reflect changes the character is experiencing.

When working with silhouettes, it is helpful to warm up your body and your face so that the energy generated from the centers will be reflected in your facial expressions.

Physical Warm-Up: Reach your arms and legs out in various directions to stretch your muscles, shake your arms and legs to loosen those muscles, bounce on your toes to vibrate your body and to loosen your trunk muscles.

Facial Warm-up: Make an exaggerated happy face, sad face, angry face and surprised face. Then switch quickly from one to another at random.

Experiment with the centers of energy: It is helpful to do these experiments moving around, changing levels (sitting, standing, kneeling, etc.).

   a. Think about something you would like to do, or something that happened to you. Engage your mind to visualize it in such detail that you become fairly unaware of your actual surroundings.

   Then switch to excitedly verbalizing details about what you have just been thinking about and visualizing.

   b. Cave in your upper chest area, restrict your breathing. What does this activity suggest might be going on in your world?

   Now, expand your upper chest, fill your upper chest with breath and see how your worldview is altered.

   c. Restrict your stomach, clench the muscles. What can you imagine might be happening to you or what sort of attitude do you feel towards the world?

   Then expand this area, taking deep, low breaths and examine how your view of the world changes. Be sure to overexaggerate these two because they reveal more with intensity.

   d. Tighten the muscles in the lower part of your body. Begin to sense how dangerous the world is around you or how overly careful you are becoming about giving yourself away to an enemy.

   Now go to the opposite extreme and have fun releasing the animal energy generated in the same area.

As you do these exercises you might feel that some of them come close to matching your habitual center of energy. That is useful information to have. One needs to be conscious of walking in one's own shoes before trying to walk in the shoes of another.

Other of these experiments may trigger memories to situations of the past. Some may be very unfamiliar and invite exploration.

USING GENDER

Be aware of the fact that there is a difference in feminine and masculine vocal ranges, postures, silhouettes, movements and gestures.

Study the differences by observing a wide range of other people.

Discover your own personal habitual movement patterns and guard against foisting them upon the characters in your stories.

Avoid stereotypical choices. A character is not only female or male but also all the other things that make up who they are. And, of course, there is a range of feminine and masculine physicality.

Underplaying gender is probably preferable to overplaying it. It is but one aspect of each character. Confusion can develop when a teller of one gender fails to change embodiment for a character of a different gender. The audience may have difficulty accepting a woman teller presenting a male if she does not adjust her body and voice to support the masculine character. Of course, the same is true for a male teller presenting a female character. The goal is *to do the portrayal with subtlety* so that attention is not drawn to what is making the portrayal believeable.

Often there will be multiple males in the story that need to be differentiated among or a combination of male and female story characters to be contrasted. Here the silhouette is invaluable. It can help trigger the physical and vocal changes needed for each character so that each can be quickly identified by the listeners.

COMMUNICATION LOOPS BETWEEN CHARACTERS

THE RELATIONSHIP WEB

Every story has a relationship web; every character in a story is connected to all other characters. In order for the teller to communicate the story he must understand all the relationships. These relationships shape the communication loops between the characters in the story.

Biblical and cultural research is necessary in order to understand the likely relationships in any story. In biblical stories, in particular, it is easy to forget that most interactions take place in the presence of other people who may not openly react, speak, or even be identified.

STORY CHARACTER POINT OF VIEW

The teller has to look through each character's point of view to understand the nature of communication occurring among the various characters. **There are no negative characters.** All characters are human and there is a wide range of humanity in the biblical stories. Individuals may do bad things in the eyes of others; but through their own eyes, they *positively* believe in their goals and feel their actions justified.

EXAMPLE STORY: "The Woman in the House of Simon the Pharisee" (Luke 7:36-47, NRSV)

One of the Pharisees asked him to eat with him, and he went into the Pharisee's house and took his place at the table.

And a woman in the city, who was a sinner, having learned that he was eating in the Pharisee's house, brought an alabaster jar of ointment. She stood behind him at his feet, weeping, and began to bathe his feet with her tears and to dry them with her hair. She continued kissing his feet and anointing them with the ointment.

Now when the Pharisee who had invited him saw it, he said to himself, "If this man were a prophet, he would have known who and what kind of woman this is who is touching him—that she is a sinner."

Jesus spoke up and said to him, "Simon, I have something to say to you." And he replied, "Speak."

"A certain creditor had two debtors; one owed five hundred denarii, and the other fifty. When they could not pay, he canceled the debts for both of them. Now which of them will love him more?"

Simon answered, "I suppose the one for whom he canceled the greater debt." And Jesus said to him, "You have judged rightly."

Then turning toward the woman, he said to Simon, "Do you see this woman? I entered your house; you gave me no water for my feet, but she has bathed my feet with her tears and dried them with her hair. You gave me no kiss, but from the time I came in she has not stopped kissing my feet. You did not anoint my head with oil, but she has anointed my feet with ointment.

Therefore, I tell you, her sins, which were many, have been forgiven; hence she has shown great love. But the one to whom little is forgiven, loves little." Then he said to her, "Your sins are forgiven."

But those who were at the table with him began to say among themselves, "Who is this who even forgives sins?" And he said to the woman, "Your faith has saved you; go in peace."

One of many relationship webs in the story:

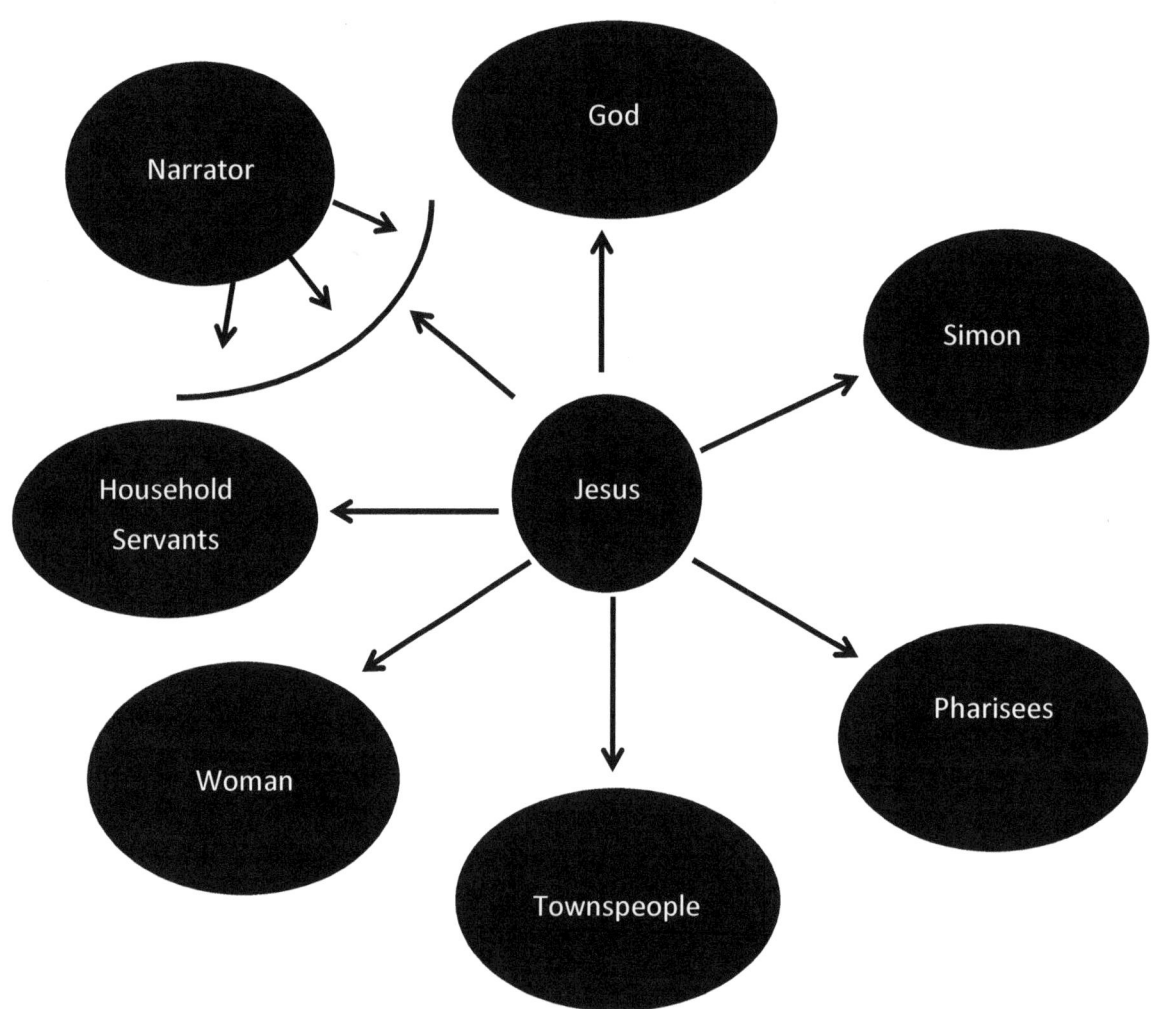

The illustration web for Jesus contains the characters present and his relationship to each of them. The relationships govern his communication loops with the various characters.

Dr. Kenneth E. Bailey discusses the story, "The Woman in the House of Simon the Pharisee," in his book *Jesus Through Middle Eastern Eyes, Cultural Studies in the Gospels*. His discussion is a must read for any biblical storyteller approaching this story. Some of the following information about the characters is gleaned from his research and discussion; all of the information represents but one possible assessment of the characters. The exercise is to make an attempt to see the event through the eyes of Jesus.

The characters surrounding Jesus in his relationship web:

God – Biblical stories are God's story, so remember to include God in the cast of characters. God is Jesus' partner; Jesus is God's spokesman.

Narrator – This is the teller of the *original* story, the witness. The narrator is the source of everything that is not in quotation marks. The narrator may be an observer at the event who is affected enough to want to tell the story. Or, the narrator may be someone who wants to tell an important story she has heard.

Simon, the Pharisee – Jesus knows full well that this man judges everyone, especially this young rabbi who has been speaking to crowds and forgiving sins. Pharisees are attempting to be the best possible Jews in their response to the presence of the Roman Empire in their country and lives. Simon has invited Jesus to his home for a meal. However, Jesus knows that there is an ulterior motive; this is not a genuine offer of table fellowship to an honored guest. It is a scheme to put this young rabbi in his place. However, Jesus can use any circumstance for teaching.

The Pharisees – These are friends and associates of Simon who also have been invited. Jesus knows that they share Simon's point of view and will back him up. Again, this might be a teaching moment.

The townspeople – Non-Pharisees, people who have been listening to Jesus and who might hope to partake of food left over from the meal. They line the walls of the room and listen to all the exchanges. For Jesus this could be an opportunity to further their understanding of his teachings.

The household servants – Those serving the food. This may be a rare opportunity for Jesus to speak in front of them.

The woman – A woman who has recognized her sin and has received forgiveness from Jesus. She was probably part of the crowd to which he was speaking earlier. He may not have even been focused on her, but she fully received his message. When his attention does move to her now, he knows that forgiveness has engendered love in her because she has positioned herself at his feet and she is holding an albastar jar of ointment, a special and dear gift. When she responds with her tears, Jesus also understands that she has seen all the slights that Simon, as host, has inflicted on him and that she feels the rebukes personally. She will be the perfect teaching tool for demonstrating the exchange ratio of forgiveness to love.

Each character has his unique relationship web. When one of the others speaks, that character moves to the center position and the connections to others are from his point of view. It is important for the teller to think about all the points of view present in the story, especially if one of those people or groups becomes vocal in the story.

SWITCHING COMMUNICATION LOOPS IN PERFORMANCE

In the example story, there are two story characters who speak and one group that speaks.

Jesus   Simon   Pharisees

When each speaks, the narrator becomes that character or group and forms the appropriate communication loop with the recipient character or group, while at the same time sharing that loop with the audience.

There are those who like to place the characters in the story in certain locations in the performance area. It is felt that this approach makes is clearer for the listener(s) to follow the action and it makes it easier for the storyteller to remember the sequence of events. While placing story characters can be a useful approach for some, it isn't necessary for everyone.

The alternative to placing characters around the performance space is simply to keep the speaking character facing the audience and move the recipient character or group to the audience. In that way, all of the listeners not only clearly see and hear all that is being communicated but also they have an opportunity to put themselves in the story and personally react as each character in the story.

Biblical stories have a different shape from the structure of drama in the Western world. Often within the story, characters do not experience a change in their point of view that is shared with the listeners. However, biblical stories can be used to affect change in the point of view of the listeners. Giving the listeners the opportunity to identify with the characters can make the result quicker and deeper.

Since the narrator usually speaks before any quoted speech, changing characters simply requires using the narration to facilitate the change from person to person in the story.

Frequently the speaking character has been identified in the narration ("Jesus said to her"). If the teller understands the characters and the communication loops necessary for them to make, switching from one speaking character to another or from story narrator to character can be effectively accomplished by the teller using changes in silhouette and voice to make the transitions clearer to the listeners.

Communication loops in the example story:

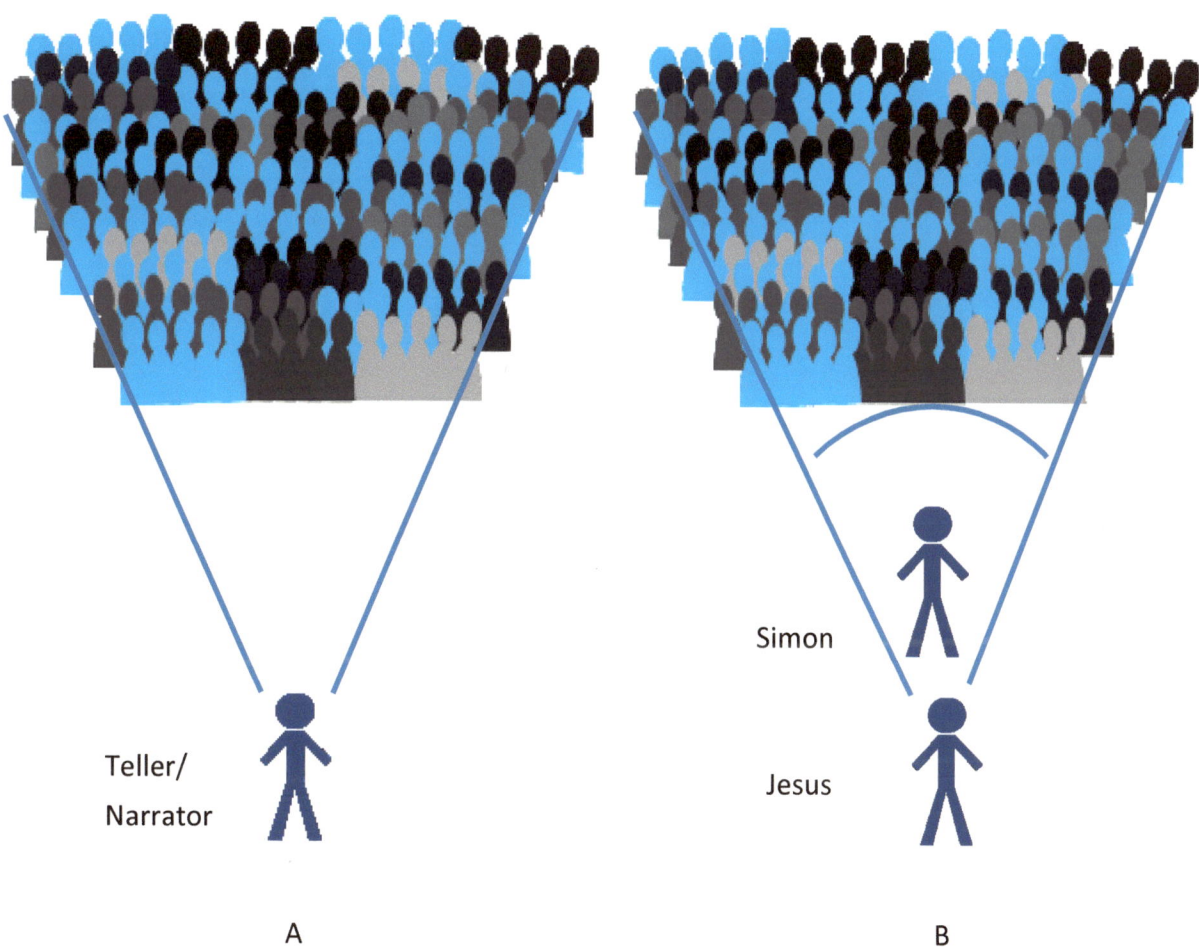

A. The teller/narrator speaks to the audience engaging each in a communication loop.

B. The narrator speaks as Jesus, addressing Simon. Note that any member of the audience can feel like they are being addressed as Simon. Each member has become part of the communication loop between Jesus and Simon. The teller does not keep her eyes fixed on one spot but treats everyone as Simon.

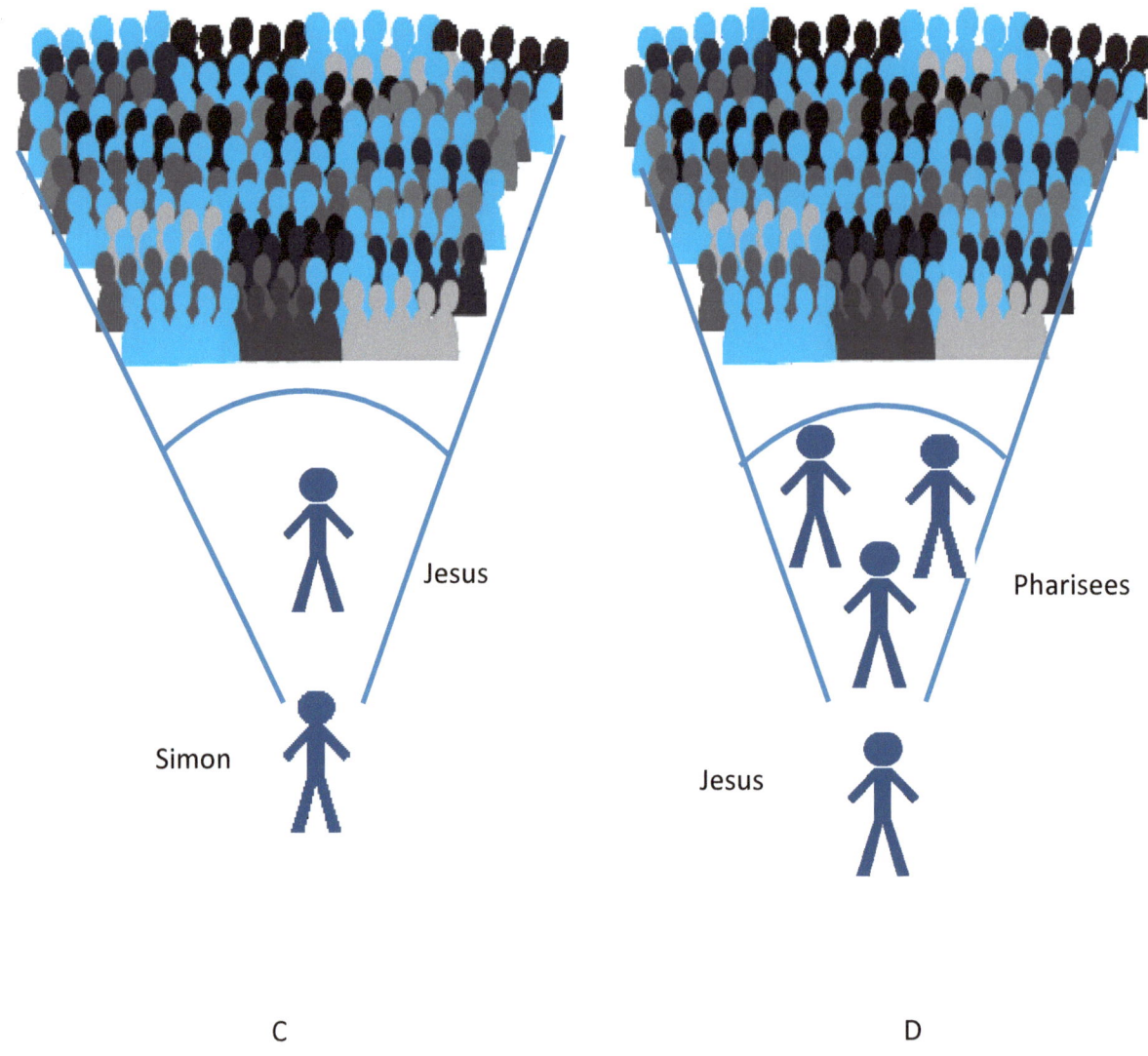

C. Now the narrator speaks as Simon, addressing Jesus. Each member of the audience has become part of the communication loop between Simon and Jesus and can experience Jesus, and thus themselves, as the recipient of what Simon is saying.

D. The narrator now speaks as Jesus, addressing the Pharisees. Each member of the audience has become part of the communication loop between Jesus and the Pharisees, now identifying as a Pharisee.

PARTING THOUGHTS

EVALUATION OF PERFORMANCE CHOICES

In order to improve as a teller, as well as to make sure you are communicating what you hope, evaluation is critical. One way to tackle the challenge is to observe your own performance.

Personally, I have a strong aversion to working in front of a mirror. In fact, I would go so far as to say that it is the poorest way of observing your own work. You cannot evaluate what you are doing as you are doing it. That is multitasking at an absurd level. How can you at the same time see the story in your mind's eye, project it before you, watch yourself performing the act of transmitting the story and be an objective observer? You simply cannot.

One approach is to watch video recordings of your performing before an audience or rehearsing before an invited audience. You can sit back and be the impartial observer. Did you receive as an audience what you thought you were transmitting as a teller? Can you see what got in the way? Did you feel as an audience the responses you desired from the audience as a teller?

Another approach is to be coached by a trusted observer who knows about the whole process, understands what you are attempting to communicate and can give you useful, supportive and insightful feedback. The method of coaching suggested by the Academy for Biblical Storytelling of the Network of Biblical Storytellers is that developed by Doug Lipman and presented in his book *The Storytelling Coach: How to Listen, Praise, and Bring Out People's Best*.

Whichever method you use for evaluation, it is essential to confront your work and challenge yourself to make more meaningful and expressive choices. Even the most experienced tellers have room for improvement; and just like our recorded voice it is often unrecognizable to us (see page 17), what we *think* we are communicating is not always what is received.

FINDING GOD ALIVE

When a biblical storyteller introduces a story, or gives historic background or context, the storyteller is the presenter of this material before she becomes the teller of the actual story. When the teller begins to tell the story she becomes the communicator through which the story comes to three-dimensional life.

The storyteller has a weighty responsibility. Research, study, prayers, experimentation, practice, life experience, control of body and use of voice all work to reclaim the life of the story. That life depends on accurate, purposeful and artistic transmission. Appendix A offers an overall approach to the process of internalizing a story for telling.

Any personal ego needs, internal censor/critic, lack of adequate preparation, or poor physical, mental and emotion health can damage the communiucation. All of this is true for any live performer committed to his or her material – a storyteller, a stage actor, a singer, a dancer, etc. A number of things might happen. A performer might draw attention to herself to the detriment of the story. He may draw laughs, but at a loss of solid communication of the story. A performer might become self-conscious, nervous and fail to keep a strong transmission open. A performer might find her physical, mental and emotional health intruding on her material or draining her resources.

Anyone can get interrupted by a distraction or lose their train of thought or stumble over a word. Those are realities in performing. But if the performer will, at that moment, refocus energy into the story, even if there is a pause, the transmission will return and the story will flow again. The important thing is not to transmit the interruption in an obvious manner to the listeners. Stay in the moment until the details return or a way out suggests itself.

Biblical storytellers have an additional responsibility and that is to be a communication device for the Holy Spirit. If one is truly communicating the story, the Holy Spirit flows through the telling. It affects how the story fills the teller, how the story penetrates the listener, how the story fills the physical performance space, how the story is received and responded to by each individual. This is exactly why a biblical storyteller goes to all the effort to prepare for the telling of a story. The point is to breathe the life back into the story and to bring it into the lives of the listeners, as well as into the life of the storyteller.

> May the words of your mouth
>
> and the meditations of your heart
>
> be acceptable in God's sight.

APPENDICES

APPENDIX A

INTERNALIZING A BIBLICAL STORY

It is always helpful to pray or to quieten your mind each time you work on the story.

Selecting a story:

You might be drawn to a particular story while reading or studying the Bible. You might be drawn to a particular person. You might be responding to a request to share a certain story or scripture. Many different things can lead you to a story.

Selecting a translation:

You can choose among various translations. There are several websites that render scriptures in multiple translations. The New Revised Standard Version is considered a sound translation from the original languages. The word choices made by other translations can often shed light on nuances in the text, as can reading the text in online inter-linear Bibles. Translator must be sensitive to the nuances in the original languages. A good translator tries to select English (for us) words that transmit more than just meaning.

Creating the script:

When you have settled on a translation, it is easiest to copy the text from an online site such as Bible Gateway which offers a wide selection of translations, and paste it into a word processing program on your computer.

When making my file copy, I note the book, chapter and verse location material at the top of the page. Then I remove all the verse numbers and footnote markings. I "select all" and put the text into an easy to read font size (for me it is 14) and I use a 1.5 setting on line spacing. Then I save the file.

Next, I read through the story dividing it into thoughts and phrases the belong together, at least seem to initially. Organization of the story is helped by using the punctuation given as a guide.

It is helpful to organize the thoughts further by separating the story into episodes. I use indentions or extra spacing to separate the different episodes on the page. This process helps provide space in the story and give you time to transition your mind and body between characters or events. These spaces also let the listeners absorb the story as it is unfolding. The beauty of living in the age of computers is that we can easily change our minds and reorganize the material on the page as we go deeper into the story. This does not mean changing the order of the story as given or an any way changing the story.

The stories were all meant to be told aloud, even the letters, which were delivered orally to groups. It can be helpful to recognize that stories are told differently in the middle-eastern and western traditions. For example, a Bible story may begin with a summary of the story followed by the particulars. It may even have summary points in the story followed by the particulars of that summary. Western tradition usually starts at the beginning and goes more linearly to the finish and the outcome of the story is not revealed until then.

It is important to keep in mind that in the Bible stories what happens is never as important as the responses of God to man and man to God.

Internalizing the script:

Now read the story from your script several times aloud.
>   Note what caught your attention; then wonder why.
>   Note anything that you wondered about or did not understand.
>   Reading the notes of a good study Bible could answer questions or give you more information.
>   Research via the Internet or books on the time period, customs, history, etc.

Read the section of Scripture before and after the story.
>   Determine where in the overall story of God this story falls.
>   You might think about why this story was included in the remembering of God's story.
>   You might consider how an original audience heard the story. What did they already know that your audience would not automatically understand?
>   You might consider how a contemporary audience will hear the story.
>   What does the contemporary audience need to know to fully hear and understand the story?

Start telling the story:

To tell the story requires you to be able to imagine the scene and things as they happen. Some people find it helpful to do a story board. Movies and video use these to lay out the images of the story's events in order. You might make a drawing for each of the episodes. These need not be works of art, but they need to include things that are important to remember in each episode. No one has to make sense of them but you.

Put down your script and try to tell the story focusing on including the important information of who, where, when and what. Do not try to get all the words exactly right and in the right order as one would with rote memorization; those details will improve as you work. See the story playing out in your mind and communicate it outside yourself. Imagine someone there listening to you. Image them responding to what you are saying. How do they respond? What has to happen as a result of each response? We communicate to be understood and to be responded to by listeners.

Go back to the script and see what you might have omitted. Try again. This is a loop you will keep making. Avoid rote memorization, that is lifeless. You might do the telling practice while walking or sitting in a rocking chair, something that lets your body have movement not specific to the story. You might tell the story in an outlandish way to avoid falling into a rut or pattern before you are ready to shape your telling. Don't settle right away on <u>how</u> you are going to do it. Let the story live inside you, let it influence you, let it speak to you, let it grow in you. **Bible stories work on you as you work on them.**

Keep asking yourself questions:
- Am I really understanding the situation?
- How do the characters differ from each other?
- How do they relate to each other?
- Do relationships change during the story?
- Who is narrating the story?
- Do I really understand everything that is happening?
- Am I communicating the differences between the narrator and each of the characters?
- Am I finding the moments of quiet or silence in the story?
- Am I finding the emotions in the story?
- **Am I finding and conveying the most important thing in the story?**
- Am I using my body and voice to help fully tell the story?

Sharing the story:
Remember that the eyes of the audience receive information faster than the ears.

It is helpful to find a practice audience or listener who will give you honest feedback. Ask them questions and see what they did not get or understand or misunderstood. Listen to their responses and think about them. Don't try to defend your choices.

You need to learn all you can about every performance space and adapt to the demands of each one so that everyone listening can both see and hear you.

The story is always God's story, given to us for God's purposes, kept alive in our world by the power of the Holy Spirit working through tellers and hearers. Let yourself be lifted on the wings of eagles in your journey.

APPENDIX B

HIDDEN POWER IN THE WORDS

English-speaking biblical storytellers need to be able to unleash the power of the words that were finally selected for any English translation. A good translator looks for the English word that most clearly and effectively reflects the overtone of the communication from all the words that mean the same thing as the word being translated.

The sounds within the words of the translated text carry as much weight as the meaning of the words. The goal is to become aware of the sounds within the text that help carry the task of completing the communication loop with listeners in the most effective manner.

In the charts on the following pages, key words (words that are usually easily pronounced) are used to demonstrate the sound/sensation associated with each number or symbol. The Lessac system identifies greater subtlety in the range of sounds used in the English language than does the International Phonetic Alphabet (IPA). The IPA is the symbol system found in dictionaries.

Remember that there are both vowels and consonants in English that can be silent within words. Example: Five friends arrived. Silent letters are not always crossed out in the following material.

Once the sounds are identified in the text, it is important to explore them freely. They can even lead you to further, deeper understanding of what you are communicating.

MAJOR VOWELS

(Lessac)   (IPA)

TONAL

y-buzz — ease   ē — even
+y-buzz — say   ā — ape

STRUCTURAL

y1 — news   yōō — use
1 — ooze   ōō — tool
21 — ode   ō — go
3 — all   ô — horn
3y — boy   oi — oil
4 — odd   ä — car
5 — alms   ä — car
51 — ounce   ou — out
6 — add   a — fat
6y — aisle   ī — bite

   Y1   5   +y   21   6   4
Yet you have made them a little lower than God,

   6   51   21   6   5
and crowned them with glory and honor.

NEUTRAL VOWELS

(Lessac)   (IPA)

N1 — took   oo — look
N2 — tick   i — is
N3 — tech   e — ten
N4 — tuck   u — up

(ə for a in ago, e in agent,
i in insanity, u in focus)

NEUTRAL DIPTHONGS

(n = N4)
N1n — poor
N2n — peer
N3n — pear
R-derivative(R̸) — bird   ər — fur

   N4 N3 N2 N2 N1n   N2
How majestic is your name in all
                   ɇ
the earth!

Note:
 Y
the earth — preceding a vowel
 N4
the heavens — preceding a consonant

CONSONANTS

VOICED: The sound is made using tone in the production.

UNVOICED: The sound is made using only breath in the production.

SUSTAINABLE: The sound is continued as long as the lips, teeth and tongue remain in the position to produce the sound.

PERCUSSIVE: The sound is made by a change in the position of the lips teeth or tongue; therefore, cannot be sustained.

COGNATES: pairs of consonants that are produced in the same way but one is voiced and the other is unvoiced.

SUSTAINABLE – VOICED		SUSTAINABLE – UNVOICED	
N	as in **n**oo**n**		
M	as in **m**i**m**e		
NG	as in si**ng**		
L	as in fi**ll**		
R	as in **r**ea**r**		

Note: The letters W, Y and H are consonants only at the beginning of a word or syllable:

W	as in **w**oe, (**w**)one		
Y	as in **y**on		
		H	as in **h**ow
V	as in **v**er**v**e	F	as in **f**i**f**e, lau**gh**
Z	as in ha**z**e, wa**s**	S	as in whiff**s**
TH	as in brea**the**	TH	as in brea**th**
ZH	as in bei**ge**	SH	as in wi**sh**

PERCUSSIVE – VOICED		PERCUSSIVE – UNVOICED	
B	as in **b**o**b**	P	as in **p**o**p**
D	as in **d**rea**d**	T	as in **t**rea**t**
G	as in **g**ro**g**	K	as in **c**oo**k**
DZ (D+Z)	as in bi**ds**	TS (T+S)	as in bi**ts**
DG (D+ZH)	as in ju**dge**	CH (T+SH)	as in **ch**ur**ch**
DL	as in fi**ddle**	TL	as in li**ttle**

CONSONANT ACTION WITHIN WORDS

SILENT: consonants that are <u>not</u> produced in preferred pronunciation or because they have become part of a vowel sound

                                  21   +y   1

of̸ten   throw   stay   through

PLAYABLE: consonants that because if their placement <u>within a word</u>, proceed another consonant to which they are not identical, a cognate or semi-related

    Sustainable   (double underline)   Percussive (single underline)

Sustainable	Percussive
ambulance	bobbed
almost	popped
songlike	madcap
lovelorn	heartfelt
lifelike	giggle
sizzling	chuckle
toothless	judgment
smooths	matchless
bashful	fiddlesticks

CONSONANT ACTION BETWEEN WORDS in CONNECTED SPEECH

CONSONANT to VOWEL

DIRECT LINK: The final consonant of one word becomes the first sound of the next word.

    Back away!   This is an arena.

CONSONANT to CONSONANT

1. PLAY AND LINK: When a consonant falls before another consonant to which it is not related, or before a pause (punctuation), there is the opportunity to go from just producing to playing the sound.

    last row   wash clean   predict when

    big man   judge not   couldn't go

        it will fit.   None comes off.

2. PREPARE AND LINK: When a consonant comes directly before another consonant to which it is identical, a cognate or semi-related, prepare the first and produce the second to avoid an unnecessary pause that will interrupt the flow of the words.

IDENTICAL	*COGNATES*	*SEMI-RELATED*
even now	keep back	help me
life force	dog collar	did this
bad judge	this zone	good news
not change	five fins	that sound

Notes: (1) Unless the speaker under-produces the letter R, it is better not to mark any letter R. (2) There is no need to mark direct linking because it occurs naturally in connected speech.

CONSONANT MARKING SAMPLE

Bless the Lord, O my soul

and do not forget all his benefits—

who forgives all your iniquity,

who heals all your diseases,

who redeems your life from the Pit,

who crowns you with steadfast love and mercy,

who satisfies you with good as long as you live

so that your youth is renewed like the eagle's.